I'M GLAD YOU'RE MY FRIEND

by VELMA SEAWELL DANIELS
illustrated by
MARY TARA O'KEEFE

The C.R. Gibson Company
Norwalk, Connecticut 06856

The other day, for the first time, I noticed those three antique keys hanging by your kitchen bulletin board. Like a lightning flash, they stirred the memory of a certain day many years ago.

I was with my mother that day when she dropped in on her best friend—your mother. I must have been five or six years old, I can't remember exactly. But, I do remember those keys. They were hanging by a string from a nail on the side of your mother's big icebox. Although I realize now that they are only about eight or nine inches long, they appeared then to be almost as long as my arm.

Your mother saw me staring at them, so she lifted them off the nail and handed them to me. "These are special keys," she said. "They were made to open the door to friendship. See what's engraved on each one. One says, 'Please,' the second one says, 'May I,' and the third says, 'Thank you.' If you always say those words when you speak to people, you will find that they are the keys to friendship. I've used them since I was a little girl. They were given to me by my grandmother."

When I saw them in your kitchen, I suddenly realized that they have been the keys to our long friendship—thanks to your great-grandmother.

Blessed are they
who have the gift of making friends,
for it is one of God's best gifts.
It involves many things,
but above all,
the power of going out of one's self,
and appreciating whatever is
noble and loving in another.

Thomas Hughes

My heart has been singing ever since the good news came. You're arriving this week! It's been so long since I've seen you. One thing for sure, we have a lot to catch up on. We can take long walks or enjoy lunch at a sidewalk cafe. There are wonderful places to visit and things to do. Or we can just sit and talk in the backyard shade and sip a glass of lemonade just as we did when we were kids. Whatever you want! Dear friend, it will be so good to see you.

I don't need a friend *like* you. I need *you*.

Your laughter and gentleness bring me great joy. You make me feel needed and wanted. When you stand beside me and show an interest in me and what I think and say and do, I feel the presence of God. And I know He sent you—to be my friend.

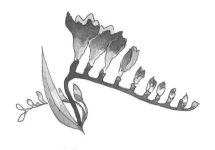

I marvel at your tireless energy, your radiance, the wonderful way you make friends feel that they are special—especially me!

I'm sorry to see you leave. Time flew, and
your visit seemed to last only a few minutes. When-
ever you come to see me, you bring so many good
moments. Laugh-a-lot-moments! You always fill
my home with happiness and sunshine. Please
hurry back.

Happy is the house
that shelters a friend.
Ralph Waldo Emerson

Last summer at the beach, I watched someone tying a boat between the mooring posts with a new nylon line. He explained that nylon is the best material to use for this purpose because it is flexible. "The line must be taut enough to keep the boat from scraping the posts," he said, "yet flexible enough so the boat can rise and fall with the waves and the tide."

Those words came to mind today when I thought of you. "That's exactly like our friendship," I said to myself. "You're dependable. I know you're ready to help, any time, anywhere, under any circumstances. I know you care, utterly. Yet, you're flexible. You are you, and you think like yourself. And in my turn I think like myself. And still we are friends."

I never considered
a difference of opinion
in politics,
in religion,
in philosophy,
as cause for withdrawing
from a friend.

Thomas Jefferson

You're like a solid rock. I've never seen you in a Sunday-mood, or a company-mood, or dinner-party-mood. Day after day, you are the same: dealing fairly, keeping your promises, and urging me to be the best I can. But above all, by your example, teaching me to put God first in everything and to build my life on His foundation.

Experienced mountain climbers never scale those dizzy heights alone. They climb in tandem, tethered one below the other, for the safety of the entire team. I'm glad I'm not climbing my mountains alone, because my link to you has made my footing sure. I hear your voice say, "Come, climb with me." And I do.

Welcome to our neighborhood! Please accept this loaf of fresh-baked wheat bread with my best wishes for a long and happy stay. I wish I could tell you that I baked it myself, but my cousin baked it for me. I'm not a gourmet cook, but I do brew a tasty cup of tea. Please come over for a visit—anytime. I hope we become friends.

Wishing to be friends is quick work,
but friendship is a slow-ripening fruit.
Aristotle

We cannot tell the precise moment when friendship is formed. As in filling a vessel drop by drop, there is at last a drop which makes it run over; so in a series of kindnesses there is at last one which makes the heart run over.

James Boswell

A potted begonia, covered with bright red blossoms, greeted me when I opened my door this morning. A little card from you read, "Hey! Did you know I was thinking of you this morning?"

What a joyful way to help me start my day. The flowers themselves will fill my room with cheer and color. And each time I glance their way I'll bless the day you moved next door to become my kind and thoughtful friend.

Nothing in my life has ever been so frustrating as trying to lose weight. Oh, those diets! Sometimes I even felt that the air I breathed was filled with calories.

Then one day you mentioned your own futile stabs at dieting. Suddenly you looked at me. "Let's diet together," you said. And for both of us, that made all the difference. Raw carrots and celery, cucumbers and sprouts seem tasty to me these days because of you. Together we are able to shun thick sandwiches of chicken and ham and Swiss cheese on rye—and yes, slathered with mayonnaise. Together we choose fruit instead of carrot cake.

Your plan is working, too. Our weight is falling. Our spirits are rising. We look better. We feel better. We are better friends, than ever. All because you said to me, "Come, take my hand and we'll walk down this rocky path together."

*The firmest friendships
have been formed in mutual adversity,
as iron is most strongly united
by the fiercest flame.*

Charles Caleb Colton

Everyone has a #1 problem-solver. You are mine. You are the best in the world because you listen to me. You never scold or seem to hint that I created the problem myself. You never shrug with indifference, or laugh at my stupidity. No matter how busy you are, day or night, you always find a moment to spare when I need you. Then, after I've cried on your shoulder, you give me a workable solution.

Yes, you are my #1 problem-solver. But, better than that, you're my friend.

The best mirror
is an old friend.
George Herbert

You are the kind of friend I want to be. You care, sympathize and understand each time I lay my tearful burdens in your lap. You never scold or preach. Even when I might be in the wrong, your hand is there for me to take. It's there to lift me up and put me right again. I like to think that maybe I'm a better friend to you and to others because you are the kind of friend you are to me.

The proper office of a friend
is to side with you
when you are in the wrong.
Nearly anybody
will side with you
when you are in the right.
                    Mark Twain

Sometimes the conversations we *don't* have
are those I remember the longest. I'm thinking now
about our side-by-side strolls through the woods.
In the spring when the pink dogwood and azaleas
are trying to outdo each other. Or the fall when the
leaves are dressed in red and yellow. And when
anything above a whisper invades our companion-
able silence.

Friends need not always chatter back and
forth. Because the real joy comes from walking
down life's paths together—just you and me.

*A friend may well be reckoned
the masterpiece of Nature.*
Ralph Waldo Emerson

*Friendship is
a sheltering tree.*
Samuel Taylor Coleridge

Oh, what I have learned from you, my calm and unruffled friend. You taught me by example without even knowing you were my tutor—my mentor.

For most of my life I fussed and fumed and got upset over the slightest mishap. With no effort, I could turn a simple blunder into a crisis or even a disaster. Then I met you. As our friendship grew, I saw how you never lost control of any situation. You once said to me, "There are only two kinds of problems. Those you can't do anything about and those you can. Let the first kind take care of themselves, and do your best to take care of the others. After that, forget it."

I laughed when you said, "Everything will come out all right," when your son scheduled his wedding the same day your daughter's baby was due—600 miles away. You were right. Your first grandchild came into the world healthy and crying, two weeks late. The problem took care of itself.

I also remember the day I drove you to the airport. If all went well, we'd be there thirty min-

utes early. But, all didn't go well. A tire blew just as we entered the four-lane highway. I nearly went to pieces. I stuttered and trembled, and did everything except scream. Then, your self-control took over. You touched me on the arm and said "Don't worry. This is one problem we *can* handle. First, it only takes fifteen minutes to change a tire. That still puts us there fifteen minutes early. Second, all we have to do is open the trunk of the car and stand there together looking helpless and some handsome man will stop and change the tire for us. Third, the plane will be late anyway."

You were right. Three minutes after we opened the trunk of the car and were trying to remove the jack, a member of my church stopped and changed the tire. And, as you said, when we arrived at the airport, we still were fifteen minutes ahead of schedule. And, again you were right—the plane was thirty minutes late.

Don't think I'm cured. Not yet! But, your example has put me on the track and shown me where I want to go.

*A friend is,
as it were,
a second self.*
Cicero

I like those days that start with a cup of coffee and a visit from you. What a delightful, friendly habit! We talk and talk and talk and talk. Sometimes we talk about a recipe or clothes or old friends. Sometimes we even gossip—just a wee bit. And always, no matter how calmly we begin, we end our morning chat with a rush and the cry, "Oh, my, look how time flies." Then, stimulated by our friendly morning communion, it's back to our daily chores.

Your adventurous invitation came at exactly the right moment. When you tapped on the window and said, "Let's go," I needed to stretch and take a break.

What a delightful break! A bicycle ride! Goodness knows I should get more exercise. But, making myself do it alone—what a boring chore.

You turned the chore into fun. In the warm sun with a breeze through your hair and a friend to ride with you, that's bicycling at its best. Thank you for routing me out, my bicycle-riding friend. Please pedal my way again—and soon.

Tuesday was my lucky day! You dropped by to sit and drink a cup of cocoa in my kitchen. What timing! That's what they call it in show business. Women call it intuition. No matter what it's called—you've got it. You know exactly when I need company.

More than that! You understand my many moods. You know when to talk and when to keep quiet, when to ask questions and when you don't dare. Sometimes you laugh, and sometimes you sympathize.

You have the gift (it's rare) to rouse and stimulate my tired and sleepy spirits. So, please come back, my wise and noble-minded friend— come back and visit me again.

*The ornament of a house
is the friends
who frequent it.*
Ralph Waldo Emerson

Oh, you dear and clever friend! You fooled me. Hook, line and sinker.

When you invited me to meet your Aunt Samantha from Sumatra, I should have known because it isn't called Sumatra anymore. Besides, in all the years I've known you, I never heard you mention any Aunt Samantha.

So, I got dressed up to meet your aunt. "Don't come until ten after eight," you said, "because I won't be home 'til then."

I rang your doorbell right on time, and there you were. "Come in and meet my aunt," you said.

I stepped inside, and then the bomb exploded. People popped up everywhere singing, "Happy Birthday."

What fun we had. The evening was filled with love and laughter.

Then, as custom dictates, it was time for me to blow out the candles on the cake and cut it so everyone could have a piece.

You brought the cake in, put it on the table, handed me the knife, and said, "Now blow!"

Right then, I knew without a single doubt what a loving, caring, gracious, and thoughtful friend you are. For in the center of the cake stood just one single candle.

Thank you.

I miss you. Not with sadness but with the joy of knowing you will soon be back with tales of distant lands and high adventure to fill those precious hours that only a special friend may share.

Your advice hit the spot. One month later, I feel better. I'm getting more accomplished with less fuss and bother, and strangely enough, I have time, now, to relax.

At first, I thought you were trying to be funny when you almost shouted at me, "You're working too hard."

Like everyone, I guess, who hears those words, I recited all my daily tasks and chores to let you know how much I have to do. You waved your hand and stopped me. "I know you have a lot to do," you said, "but when you do it, don't work hard—work smart."

Then you showed me how you list tomorrow's schedule on your memo pad at night and suggested I give it a try. "Put everything in order," you explained, "and don't forget to add that walk around the block and mark the phone call to a friend. The walk will give you time to think. The visit with your friend will lift your spirits."

You saw me when I needed help, and gave it. Because you are my friend, I took it. And so—God blessed both of us!

When I popped in on you the other day, I meant to bring a little cheer and comfort. Instead, I came away renewed and lifted up and filled with joy because of you.

I found you busy, caring for a loved one. For weeks and weeks, you've hardly slept a full night through, and yet you never gave a hint that you were tired. And as you went about your chores, you smiled and even laughed and brought a touch of sunshine to the sickroom.

No words of gloom or dire complaint were heard from you, but only those of faith and hope and love. And while you spread good cheer throughout your home, a bit of it rubbed off on me and made me proud that I can call you *friend*.

You always say to me, "Be sure to call me if you need me." And I do. You hear from me when the cat is sick, or the sink's clogged up. I call you when it's good news, bad news, a bit of gossip, or maybe just a problem. Big problem, little problem, they're all the same to you. Some you can solve, most you can't. But, mainly you listen. Mainly you are there.

I'm glad you're there.
I'm glad you're my friend.

If only I could, I would change yesterday for you. Of course, no one can do that. I pray that your heartache will be less by tomorrow, but I am concerned about today. Please know that I am here to help make today as endurable for you as possible. And if you need me tomorrow, I will be here for you, too.

*The most I can do
for my friend
is simply to be
his friend.*
Henry David Thoreau

If I were writing your biography, I would title it, "*Zest!*" Just one word, *zest*. Because that fits you better than any ten or twenty words I could string together.

My dictionary gives this definition for zest: "*Added flavor or interest; spirited enjoyment.*" At first I thought zest could be compared to the icing on a cake. Not so! Zest is more than that. Every cake worthy of the name is covered with icing. Zest would be the colorful flowers and fancy decorations on top of the icing—that extra touch.

I remember the time I gave a dinner party for a few close friends. When I invited you, I told you who else would be there. You arrived a few minutes early that evening so you could arrange the placecards you had made as a surprise for me. You had used your calligraphic skill to letter each one and then had decorated it with a tiny coquina shell, spread out and glued down to look like a butterfly. *Zest!*

Any time you come into a room, the place lights up. The way you smile, the way you talk, the way you listen electrifies the very air. *Zest.*

And when we chance to meet, at your house, my house, or on the street, you do the same to me. You sparkle. Your cup of joy overflows and spills all over me. And when you've said goodbye, I find you've always left behind a spot of *zest*.

*A **true friend is
forever a friend.***
George MacDonald

What can I say?

How can I thank a friend? How can I thank you for quietly slipping into the pew beside me in church each Sunday? How can I thank you for laughing at my silly jokes when I try to be funny? How can I thank you for tending my African violets when I'm out of town? How can I thank you for being so thoughtful and gracious and kind? How can I thank you for being my friend?

What can I say—except "*thank you.*"

Book design by Laura Hough
Type set in ITC Garamond